Life in the Time of
The First Americans
Revised Edition

Lisa Trumbauer

capstone

© 2008, 2016 Heinemann Library
an imprint of Capstone Global Library, LLC. Chicago, Illinois

To contact Capstone Global Library, please
call 800-747-4992, or visit our web site
www.capstonepub.com

**Library of Congress Cataloging-in-Publication Data
is available on the Library of Congress website.**
ISBN 978-1-4846-4013-5 (revised paperback)
ISBN 978-1-4846-3502-5 (ebook)

Photo Credits
Bridgeman Images: Detroit Institute of Arts/Gift of Mrs Blanche Ferry Hooker, 18, Peter Newark American Pictures, 23; Getty Images: Encyclopaedia Britannica/UIG, 10, MPI, 26, 27; iStockphoto: SkyF, 22; Library of Congress: Cover Bottom, Cover Top, 5, 24, 25; Mapping Specialist: 4, 6, 7; North Wind Picture Archives: 15, 19; Shutterstock: Andrea Izzotti, 11, Bill Kennedy, 20, Critterbiz, 21, Elizabeth C. Zurek, 16, Sara Winter, 8, Sekar B, 9, Steve Bower, 14, sumikophoto, 12, turtix, 17, visuelldesign, 13

Map illustrations on pages 4, 6, and 7 by Mapping Specialists, Ltd.

Cover photograph of the landing of Christopher Columbus reproduced with permission of Getty Images. Cover photograph of oil on canvas of Indian braves hunting deer by Joseph Henry Sharp reproduced with permission of Private Collection, Photo © Christie's Images/The Bridgeman Art Library.

The consultant for this book was Isabel Tovar. She is the Collections Manager and NAGPRA Coordinator for the Anthropology Department at the Denver Museum of Nature and Science.

Printed and bound in the USA.
009878R

Contents

Some words are shown in bold, **like this**. You can find out what they mean by looking in the glossary.

The First Americans

People have lived in America for thousands of years. Scientists think the first people walked to America from Asia. Thousands of years ago, Asia and **North America** were **joined** together.

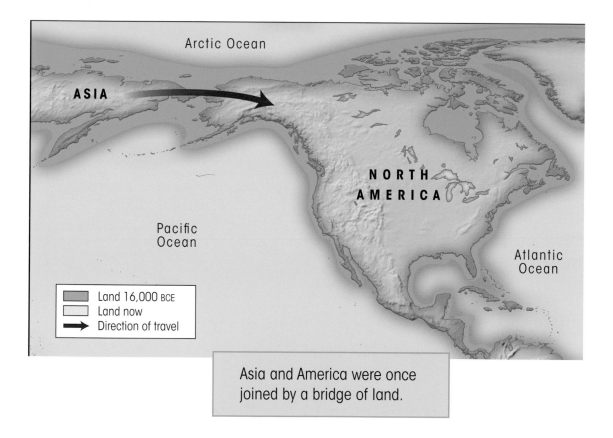

Asia and America were once joined by a bridge of land.

Most first Americans lived in large groups.

Over time, millions of Native Americans lived in America. Native Americans are people who first lived in North America. They lived in forests, deserts, and places in between. They learned how to live with the things nature gave them.

Before the United States

The United States is the name of a country. The United States is on the **continent** of **North America**. A continent is a very large piece of land. North America has three large countries: Canada, the United States, and Mexico.

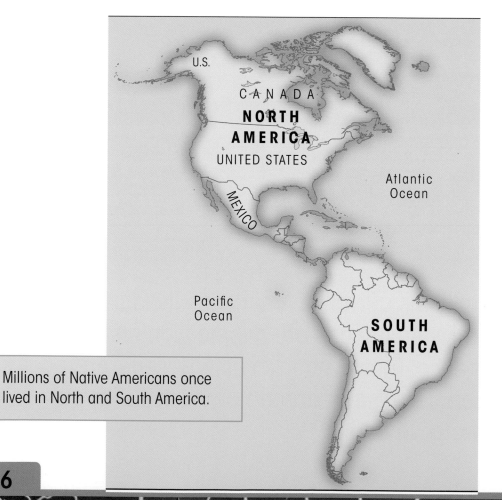

U.S.

CANADA

NORTH AMERICA

UNITED STATES

MEXICO

Atlantic Ocean

Pacific Ocean

SOUTH AMERICA

Millions of Native Americans once lived in North and South America.

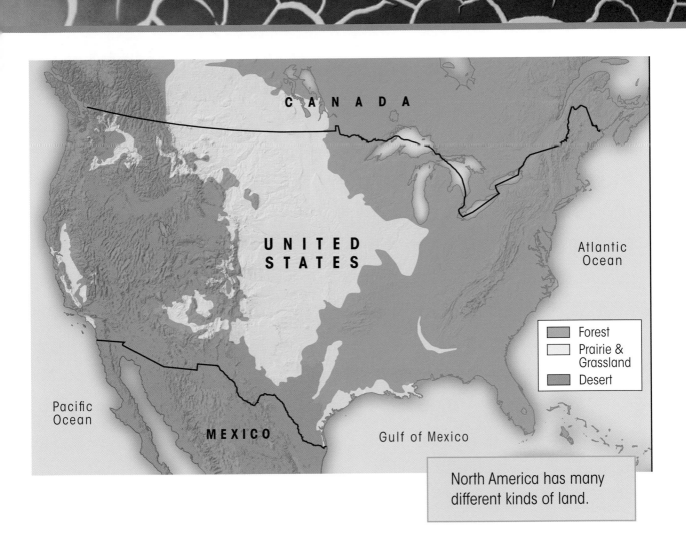

North America has many different kinds of land.

Thousands of years ago, the United States, Canada, and Mexico did not exist. The first Americans did not have countries. Instead, they lived within their own groups (also called tribes or nations). They followed their own **traditions**.

Lands of the Northwest

The land of the northwest is covered with forests. It is bordered by the Pacific Ocean, and many islands line the **coast**. The weather is rainy, but not too cold. It is the perfect place for many plants and animals to live and grow.

Some forests, like this one, are called rain forests.

The ocean and rivers are full of animals such as salmon and shellfish. The plants grow things that people and animals can eat such as berries and nuts. Many trees in the northwest grow tall and strong.

Salmon spend part of their life in a river and part in the ocean.

People of the Northwest

Canoes made from trees helped the first Americans travel.

The northwest was a perfect place for first Americans to live. They had plenty of fish and animals to eat. They also had plenty of plants to eat. They didn't need to grow their own food.

Many totem poles show animal figures.

Many first American groups there carved **totem** poles. The poles were made from trees. Some Native Americans today still carve totem poles. Some Native Americans that still live in the northwest are the Chinook and the Haida.

Deserts of the Southwest

A desert is a place that gets very little rain. Most deserts are hot, dry places. Not many plants can grow there. Some deserts are sandy. Other deserts have tall cliffs and deep **canyons**.

This area in the southwest is called Monument Valley.

Rattlesnakes hide in the cool shade of desert rocks.

Animals and plants find ways to live in the southwest deserts. Some plants, such as cactuses, don't need a lot of water. Animals find **shelter** in the rocks and under the ground. Some animals sleep during the hot day and come out at night when the air is cooler.

People of the Southwest

These cliff dwellings are in Colorado.

The first Americans had to learn how to live in the desert. The Anasazi (also called Hisatsinom) built their homes on the sides of cliffs. These cliff **dwellings** were **communities**. The cliffs **protected** them from bad weather and enemies.

The Anasazi are the **ancestors** of the Puebloan Native Americans.

The Anasazi left their cliff dwellings around the year 1300. Scientists think a big **drought** came and very little rain fell. The Anasazi did not have any food. They moved south, deeper into the desert.

Prairies of the Midwest

Prairies are large areas of land covered by grass. Prairies are also called grasslands. Not many trees grow on the prairie. Long ago, prairies covered much of the middle of **North America**.

Prairies today are not as big as they were hundreds of years ago.

Many animals lived on the midwest prairie. One of the biggest prairie animals was the buffalo. The buffalo lived in big herds and ate the prairie grasses. Buffalo have warm, shaggy coats.

Today most buffalo live on **protected** lands, like parks.

People of the Midwest

Some first Americans of the prairie built homes called **tepees**.

Many first American groups lived on the prairie. They are called the Plains Native Americans. Some Plains groups that still live in the midwest are the Comanche, the Omaha, and the different Sioux groups.

The buffalo was important to the first Americans. They hunted the buffalo for food. They made homes, clothes, and shoes from buffalo **hide**. They made tools from buffalo bones.

First Americans killed only the buffalo they needed.

Forests of the North

Long ago, many parts of **North America** were covered with forests. In the north, the forests change with the seasons. The trees are green and leafy in the summer. Some trees have no leaves in the winter.

In the fall, the leaves of some trees change colors.

Black bears find food and shelter in a forest.

Then, as now, many animals lived in the forest. The trees make good homes for animals such as raccoons and opossums. Deer also find **shelter** there. Rivers make good homes for beavers.

People of the North

Many families lived in an Iroquois home called a longhouse.

Many first American groups lived in the forests of the north and along the east **coast**. One group was the Iroquois. The forests had everything the Iroquois needed. The Iroquois built homes from the trees.

The Iroquois grew food in their gardens.

The Iroquois lived in **communities**. The communities had **longhouses** and gardens. The Iroquois hunted animals and gathered plants in the forest for food. Today some Iroquois groups still live in the north.

Strangers Arrive!

In 1492 a man named Christopher Columbus left the **continent** of Europe. He sailed across the Atlantic Ocean. He stopped on the islands, just off the **coast** of **North America**.

Christopher Columbus was born in Italy, a country in Europe.

People in Europe did not know about America. They wanted to see what was there. They wanted to **claim** America as their own. They were surprised to find that people lived there.

The first Americans met Columbus and his crew in 1492.

Change Is Coming

First Americans who lived along the east **coast** met the Europeans first.

The Europeans were different from the first Americans. Their **traditions** and beliefs were different. Their language and clothing were different. The Europeans wanted to own the land.

More and more people from Europe came to America. The first Americans did not understand these people. They did not understand how people could own the land. The way of life of the first Americans was about to change forever.

Many more ships from Europe arrived in America.

If You Grew Up Long Ago

If you grew up in the time of the first Americans…

- You would have to hunt and gather your own food.

- You would not have a refrigerator to keep your food fresh.

- You would have to make your clothes from animal skins and plants.

- You would not have books to read.

- You probably would not go to school, but you would learn from the people around you.

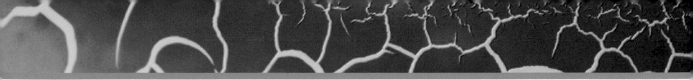

Timeline

Around

16,000 BCE People from Asia walk into **North America**.

1200 CE Anasazi build cliff **dwellings**.

1300 CE Anasazi leave their cliff dwellings and move south.

1492 CE Christopher Columbus lands on islands off the **coast** of North America.

How to Say It

Anasazi: ah-nuh-SAH-zee

Chinook: sheh-NOOK

Comanche: keh-MAN-chee

Haida: HYE-dah

Hisatsinom: he-SOT-see-nohm

Iroquois: EAR-eh-koiy

Omaha: OH-meh-hah

Sioux: sue

Find Out More

Books

Ansary, Mir Tamim. *Eastern Woodlands Indians*. Chicago: Heinemann Library, 2000.

Koestler-Grack, Rachel A. *The Sioux: Nomadic Buffalo Hunters*. Mankato, MN: Capstone, 2003.

Wade, Mary Dodson. *Christopher Columbus*. New York: Children's Press, 2003.

Williams, Suzanne Morgan. *Chinook Indians*. Chicago: Heinemann Library, 2003.

Wolfson, Evelyn. *Native Americans*. Milwaukee, WI: Gareth Stevens, 2005.

Internet Sites

FactHound offers a safe, fun way to find Internet sites related to this book. All of the sites on FactHound have been researched by our staff

Visit www.fachound.com

Glossary

ancestor person in a family that lived a long time ago

canyon very long, deep valley with cliffs

claim say that something belongs to you

coast land next to the ocean

community group of people that live in the same place

continent one of seven very large pieces of land on Earth

drought period of time with very little rain

dwelling place to live; home

hide animal skin

join come together; connect

longhouse Native American home made from trees

North America one of the seven continents on Earth

protect keep safe from danger

shelter place to stay safe from the weather

tepee Native American home made out of animal skin, shaped like a cone

totem tree carved to look like animals and other things found in nature

tradition custom and belief passed down from parents to children

Index